WORD PLAY

MOTION WORDS

lead

waddle

follow

by Carrie B. Sheely

PEBBLE
a capstone imprint

Throw! Swing! Catch!

How are these words alike?
They all tell you about action!
Are you ready to learn some
motion words?

Let's go!

throw

cartwheel

somersault

flip

push

nudge

yawn

stretch

skip

spray

spray

spray

spray

hang

grab

fall

toss

juggle

pant

pant

pant

play

climb

cuddle

dive

crash

waddle

follow

What other motion words do you see?

hurry

rush

mush

run

run

slide

run

pull

run

What other motion words do you see?

launch

lift

flow

erupt

splash

splash
splash

float

splash

splash

Pebble Sprout is published by Pebble,
an imprint of Capstone.
1710 Roe Crest Drive
North Mankato, Minnesota 56003
www.capstonepub.com

**Library of Congress Cataloging-in-Publication Data
is available on the Library of Congress website.**
ISBN: 978-1-9771-1313-9 (library binding)
ISBN: 978-1-9771-1829-5 (paperback)
ISBN: 978-1-9771-1319-1 (eBook PDF)

Summary: Through engaging photos,
introduces action verbs.

Image Credits
Shutterstock: 3Dsculptor, 28–29, Alex Kravtsov, 2,
Aneese, 20, Aspen Photo, 3 (top), Beate Wolter, 6–7,
Ben Schonewille, 3 (bottom), bez_bretelky, 9, DenisNata,
16, englishinbsas, 11, fboudrias, 29 (top), First Class
Photos PTY LTD, 4, gillmar, 26–27, gpointstudio, 17, Greg
Brave, 18 (bottom), Ivan Kovbasniuk, 12–13, Kaia92, 14
(top), Lumppini, 25, Maggy Meyer, 19, Maila Facchini, 14
(bottom), Mandy Godbehear, 10, Master1305, cover, Mikhail
Bakunovich, 24, Mr.Popz Photo, 1, NaturesMomentsuk,
22–23, Olesia Bilkei, 8, Robert Kneschke, 5 (top), Ruslan
Shugushev, 5 (bottom), sanjagrujic, 15, Tobie Oosthuizen,
18 (top), Walter Singleton, 7 (bottom), Wolfilser, 21,
zagorodnaya, 30–31

Editorial Credits
Designer: Juliette Peters
Media Researcher: Svetlana Zhurkin
Production Specialist: Katy LaVigne

Printed and bound in the USA.
PA99

Titles in this set: